Their Face, Your Business

Tracey Dennison

ACKNOWLEDGMENTS!

This book has been a complete labour of love and would not have been possible without the support and help of my biggest cheerleaders.

Huge thanks to my wonderful husband, fabulous boys, the brilliant Lorraine and amazing Lisa. You are all incredible and I am so grateful for your belief in me.

Love always xxx

CONTENTS

	Acknowledgements	i
1	Introduction	6
2	Discover your 'why'	10
3	Getting started, the practicalities	16
4	What to expect in the early days	23
5	Why mindset matters in business	30
6	Getting in a good place	35
7	Make some space	40
8	Pay attention	46
9	Getting clear on your direction of travel	53
10	Marketing	59
11	Practicalities	73
12	Developing a winning mindset	78
13	Daily routines for a positive mental attitude	89
14	Inspired action	96
15	Fear and overwhelm	100
16	Setting boundaries	107
17	Refresh, reflect, renew	114
18	Keep in touch	119
19	Additional recommended reading/listening	121

Their Face, Your Business

FOREWORD

I am honored to be providing a foreword for this book 'Their Face, Your Business', and feel it a privilege to have been asked.

As a practicing law of attraction & mindset coach I really do believe that both mindset and strategy are key components to creating a successful business and from reading this book I think the author, Tracey Dennison has beautifully described this ... Showing how start-up strategy is essential, but also that the mindset behind the work is the game changer to achieving success.

Let me introduce the author Tracey Dennison and why this book is perfect for not only those who are starting out within the aesthetics industry, but also those who have been in the business for a while and are wanting to scale their results.

I met Tracey just under 12 months ago and at this point she already had an established business within the aesthetics industry that she runs alongside her NHS commitments. At the time of meeting Tracey, she already showed great leadership within building her own business. She has built up and held a good aesthetic client base. She shares in this book her experience and expertise of the 'how', 'the strategy' behind this success. This knowledge is sure to save the reader of the book wasted time, energy, resources and finances, resulting in faster results in growing their business. It was clear to me that Tracey was an expert within her business industry. With a strong work ethic and a desire for a high level of patient care, Tracey had created a sustainable business through the business start-up strategies she shares with you in this book. However, she was ready to take her business to the next level.

Here is where the missing link came in to play - this missing link was the mindset behind strategy. As a previous mental health nurse and now a mindset coach for female entrepreneurs, I found out many years ago the important role that mindset plays in someone's life - of someone succeeding with their goals or not, to someone feeling joy or not, to someone feeling fulfilled or not. In anything we do in life, mindset and creating a positive mindset is paramount to success.

Working with Tracey and seeing her bring the mindset element into her own business, has seen her business grow with huge momentum, seeing a 300% business growth in the last 2 years. I am very excited that Tracey has now decided to support others within the aesthetic industry in growing their own business, using both strategy and mindset. I believe these two components woven together is essential in Creating long term success, and Tracey has seen her own business grow by bringing in the mindset work to her daily practice.

Tracey without a doubt is the perfect person to be the author of this amazing book, 'Their Face, Your Business' because she has first-hand experience of the success both elements bring into business. She has the experience and expertise in both start up business strategy and mindset growth. She has gone through the ups and downs of starting up her own business, created a sustainable and profitable business. She has then developed her own skills, understanding and expertise of growth mindset within business success and applied such to great effect.

Everything that she shares within this book is sure to

help someone who follows her guidance, create their own successful and profitable aesthetic business. It has been both refreshing and rewarding to have worked with Tracey, to see her own business grow. To see her weave the two elements of start-up strategy and mindset into this book is very exciting.

In summary, the key to success is not just within the strategy but within the daily mindset shifts and metaphysical tools that one brings into their life and business. Tracey explains all this well, with ease and practicality to help another aesthetic practitioner succeed. Tracey really is a pioneer within applying the mindset and strategy into building a successful aesthetic business.

Enjoy reading this book, 'Their Face, Your Business'. I am sure you will find it of immense value to growing your own successful business through strategy and mindset.

Much love

Lisa McMurtry

Law of Attraction & Mindset Coach for the Female Entrepreneur

1 INTRODUCTION

Aesthetics, it is a funny old business to be in! There are a huge number of practitioners out there and it is a massively growing industry so what makes a successful business model? What are you bringing to the table which sets you apart? Why should patients choose you?

As a Nurse of many, many years and a business woman for several of those, I have done all of the things; I invested hugely in developing my clinical skills, sought all the right advice for accountancy, technology and business management and threw myself 100% into making it work. I have had great success over time through doing this but gaining patients into the practice was a 'slow burn' and very much like many of my colleagues in the business it took 2-3 years to break even, this is totally normal with any new business in pretty much any industry. Just to be clear from the beginning, Medical Aesthetics is not an area where you will achieve overnight financial success; it will take you time to create a profitable, successful business.

From the beginning, I worked hard to establish my practice, but still felt something was missing so, I decided to invest in some mindset coaching. This, for me, has been an absolute game changer. I have learned how vital the right mindset is, what that mindset looks like for me (it is not a one size fits all scenario), how to achieve it and even more importantly how to maintain it. There are many forms of 'mindset' coaching in the business world and I had put my toes in the water of several before I went 'all in'. Although some of these mindset or business coaches had very valid things to say, their style was not really for me, some felt quite aggressive and others too 'airy fairy'. As an eternal pragmatist I needed something I could rationalise my thinking from, something based on common sense, with an evidence base and most importantly, something which worked for me. I think I've now found it! It is important to note though that as you grow and develop within your own business, your needs change. The coaching which did not work for me initially may well be exactly what is required further along in the journey. Everything has its place, do not write anything off unless it makes you feel really uncomfortable. It is about finding the best fit and what inspires you right now.

Within these pages I would like to guide you through how the clinical, business, management and mindset elements of taking off in medical aesthetics, weave together to create a thriving business, attracting the kind of patients you want to treat. All whilst keeping your stress to a minimal level, your feet firmly on the ground and a smile on your face.

The first few chapters of this book look at the logistics of getting started in your aesthetics business. For those with a more established practice however, there may still be useful nuggets within the 'start-up' pages; helpful information I wish I had known at the beginning which did not dawn on me until much further down the road.

After the practicalities of commencing a 'start-up', we take a look at the mentoring, coaching and mindset aspects of business, which can be applied wherever your business progression currently sits. This aspect of development is an iterative process; forever evolving and changing and somewhat cyclical. The elements can be taken individually but yield the greatest results when combined together in a big picture approach.

So, welcome, come on in, get comfy and hold on tight! there's work to be done!

2 DISCOVER YOUR 'WHY'

So, this is the big one, huge in fact. This is your reason for being in business and your anchor to keep going. Your 'why' needs to be emotional, it isn't something like 'I have my business to make money'; money is a result, not a reason. It can take time to discover your 'why' and could be something you need to sit with and work on for a while before you really feel it.

One simple way of finding your 'why' is to work backwards from the obvious things and challenge yourself (or even better, work this through with a group of those invested in your business) until you get to the root of the issue for example:

- Why do you want to start this business?

    o   To make money

- Okay, so why do you need to make money?

    o   To provide for my family

- Why do you need to provide for your family?

    o   Well because without my money they won't have food, clothes, a house etc

- So, are you saying your 'why' is because you love your family and want to do everything you can to make sure they are healthy, happy and well looked after, in which case is the 'why' for 'love, health and happiness'?

The example above is simplified and brief but explains a little how it is possible to narrow down the imagined output to get to the crux of what is driving the individual in this particular case. The example uses love and a sense of responsibility as the overall 'why' which will be the cornerstone (in this example) of the business.

Discovering your individual 'why' is also so much more than your anchor (although this is a pretty essential thing when times are tough and we wonder why on earth we are in this crazy business!) Very often 'why' can be the cornerstone of your business too.

Look at some of the major players and how they use their 'why' in their marketing. As an example, Apple have the tag line 'think different'. Rolls Royce have a vision of 'providing a sanctuary of calm in an ever-faster world'. Louis Vuitton talks about representing 'the most refined around the world ... synonymous with both elegance and creativity'. Consider Disney bringing us 'the happiest place on Earth', even MacDonalds are 'lovin' it'! All of these visions stem from the original 'why' and are brilliant examples of how focusing on your passion and representing emotions, rather than selling a product or service, have proven to be dramatically successful marketing strategies as well as keeping the organisation focused on the original 'why'.

Another important point to note is that the most successful businesses have an outward looking 'why'. For example, 'I love to help my patient find their sense of self and their confidence'; my reason for being as a business is centred totally around that. My 'why' is outward looking not self-focused, I consider other people and what I can do for them to be the focal point in my business strategy. I very much doubt that my business would be as successful as it is, if the focus was myself. Consider again the marketing strategies of the big players previously mentioned. All of them are looking towards those they serve rather than serving themselves. Perspective is everything here, where does yours lean towards?

So, before you start investing in the practicalities of business development, which will take time, effort, money and possibly blood, sweat and many tears, find your 'why'. Hold onto it, make it your raison d'être, weave it into the fibre of everything else in your business and make it your grounding when faced with uncertainty, adversity or any other challenges. From this you will have an excellent cornerstone to build on and something to keep your feet on the ground for and allow your business to fly.

As business evolves our 'why' can change, so remember to revisit this from time to time. If you find yourself in the amazing position of being a six-figure business your original 'why' may have lost some of its relevance. You may need to reframe your statement slightly to reflect your new financial status however, it is likely the essence of your 'why' will have remained similar to the original ethos. Often, it is just the way we communicate this which requires some adjustment over time.

Finally, do not underestimate the power of sharing your 'why' and looking for ways to measure if you are staying true to your ethos. Many medical aesthetic businesses start with a solo Dr, Nurse or Dentist and it can be difficult to see the bigger team. They are there though, take a look. Who are your biggest cheerleaders (family/friends?), where do you contract work to (formally or informally) eg, accountancy, website etc? Really, anyone involved in the business needs to understand the motivators, the ethos and direction of travel. With this information they can support, guide, mentor, direct and understand your challenges. They can celebrate the wins (and you must, every one of them – more on this later) and help you find the lessons and learnings when plans go awry. Gather your tribe, communicate, celebrate and move forward safe in the knowledge you have an amazing 'why'!

Personal Stories: It took me a long time to figure out my 'why'. I fell into Aesthetics a bit by accident and never expected to love it as much as I do. My reason for starting in aesthetics was really to support a friend so although my reasons were outward looking it was not something I had thought about too much. I totally did not expect to fall in love with the industry and had no concept of the positive impact good treatments can have on patients and how that would light me up in return.

It wasn't until I engaged with some coaching myself that I realised how important this is and honestly, it still took me a long time to figure it out. It was actually my business coach (fabulous woman!) who helped me articulate my 'why' following lengthy discussions where she teased out all of the component parts which combine together to form my drive, focus and passion. It took weeks really for me to begin to understand my own 'magic formula'. It's quite an exciting process to go through and you'll know when you have properly defined your own why; something just clicks in a 'yes, that's it' kind of moment!

3 GETTING STARTED; THE PRACTICALITIES

Getting started can be tricky, my top advice would be, do not allow yourself to procrastinate too much. There is a temptation to wait until you have designed the perfect business cards, printed beautiful brochures and got everything just perfect; this can take a long time, a very long time, by which point you might feel doubts creeping in, enthusiasm beginning to wane and the vibe takes a downturn. There are however, a huge number of things to consider:

- o Training – make sure you have done your homework about your training provider ensuring you are taught by medically qualified practitioners who are also certified trainers. Check their feedback, reviews and post-training support programme.

- Insurance – make sure you have indemnity insurance for your practice and that it covers the products that you are using.
- You may also need public liability insurance depending on your planned business premises, make sure you are aware if you need it, failure to do so could end up being a very expensive omission.
- Start-up kit – know where you can source the kit you will need and how much this will all cost.
- Emergency kit – in order to practice safely you must have a properly equipped emergency kit. You can organise this as individual items or just buy a full kit from the Aesthetics Complications Expert group (for UK based practitioners). This is an amazing group to belong to and worth its weight in gold if you need help with a serious complication.
- Where will you practice from? Do you have access to a clinic room? what are the associated expenses?
- Do you need a prescriber?
- Do you need an accountant?
- Have you sorted a website and social media accounts; do you need support with this or can you manage it in-house?

- o Do you need to develop any strategic partnerships?
- o Do you know what treatments you are offering and have a plan or formula for price setting?
- o How much are you expecting to invest in further training/education per year.
- o Depending upon your treatment offerings, do you need equipment to enable you to do these? Have you got appropriate insurance/support in place to use the products?
- o Do you need to be CQC registered? (some procedures demand that you are).
- o Do you need to source a mentor to support you in the early days and help you consolidate your training?
- o Have you got all the appropriate policies and procedures integral to your organisation? Several of the Aesthetic groups (eg the Private Independent Aesthetic Practitioners Association/British Association of Cosmetic Nurses) can provide templates for you to adopt and adapt which can be really helpful.
- o Have you registered your business with Companies House?
- o Will you be a sole trader or limited company?

- o How will patients contact you; do you need a business phone line or mobile number?
- o Which social media accounts do you need to set up?
- o Make sure you are registered with at least one reputable aesthetics pharmacy.
- o Understand what sundries you need and how much they cost (dressing packs, skin preparation, needles, syringes, do you need a fridge etc).
- o Register with the Information Commissioner's Office (mandatory if you are keeping personal details eg patient records). See www.ico.org.uk

Consideration of all of the above is important but try not to over complicate this process. Keep things as easy and simple as possible; there are plenty of complexities that must be dealt with so do not over complicate anything if it is not totally necessary.

Most importantly make sure you are practicing safely and within the remit of the industry rules. There are strict standards around prescribing (spoiler alert; it is face to face, every time prior to issuing a prescription for Botulinum Toxin) and there are also strict advertising standards for the industry.

The Advertising Standards Association's 'Blue Guide' is a must read as falling foul of this could land you in big trouble:
https://assets.publishing.service.gov.uk/government/uploads/system/uploads/attachment_data/file/824778/Blue_Guide.pdf

Personal Stories: It took me a long time to get properly started in the world of Medical Aesthetics. I'll be honest, at times I panicked because the bookings were just not happening. During the first few (slow) months, at a point when I was particularly vulnerable, I managed to get completely scammed and set myself back months financially. I'm sharing this to hopefully try and prevent others from making the same mistake...

I was feeling anxious and scared. I had invested several thousand pounds of our (family) savings into my business to cover the costs of training, insurance and equipment but business was slow. At this point I was cold called, on my business number, by a 'Facebook Marketing Expert' who promised me everything. He said he would increase my social media following, my bookings would go through the roof, in fact I'd probably be asking them to 'dial things down' I'd be so busy! They knew all about the aesthetics industry and advertising laws, oh, and they wouldn't take on another similar business within a 20-mile radius to ensure all their hard work directed patients to me. It all sounded too good to be true (that is a red flag, right there) however, in my vulnerable, scared state of mind it seemed like a good thing to try. This chap emailed documentation over whilst I was on the phone and I signed up. Almost the second I put the phone down, I realised I had been scammed. I Googled the name of the business who had approached me and confirmed my worst fears.

I tried to cancel my arrangement, but it turns out, if you are a business, there is no 'cooling off' period required in law, so that was a non-starter. I ended up losing upwards of £600 at a time when I had only small numbers of patients on my books. I did at least have the foresight to set up duplicate social media pages (the scammers needed administration rights to these in order to advertise for me) so no-one else could access my original social media sites. This business did do a small amount of advertising for me (it involved copying my posts from my original social media sites onto the ones I'd set up for this business to access). Needless to say, patients were not knocking down the door to book, there was never any question of having to 'dial down' their influence and I deleted the related social media accounts as soon as I could discontinue my association with said scammers (approximately 2 months).

The moral of the story is simple, if it sounds too good to be true, it probably is. There are no shortcuts in business. Do the work and when you are not working in your business, work on your business. Do not expect miracles but if you work hard and follow the principles in this book, the patients will come and they will be great and loyal assets to your business. Do not panic, give yourself time, give yourself credit for all the progress you do achieve, your time will come.

4 WHAT TO EXPECT IN THE EARLY DAYS

Please do not be labouring under the illusion that practicing in aesthetics is a quick fix for easy money, it absolutely is not. Expect to invest a minimum of around £3000 to get started but this figure could be significantly more. Gaining paying patients through your door can take a long time. Generally, in this industry, aesthetic treatments are not particularly discussed by patients (although there are exceptions to this and these people can really help your business if you look after them well). Referrals can be slow; patients are unlikely to venture your way until you have built yourself a solid reputation and therefore the initial months can leave you feeling a little deflated and wondering why you started.

It is at this point many practitioners throw in the towel with the view of 'well it just didn't happen for me'. Be assured, success in the industry doesn't 'just happen' for any of us. It can take years of perseverance to build up a steady stream of patients and a reputation in your area. It takes the average practitioner 2-3 years to break even; is it worth it? Well, in my opinion, yes, it absolutely is but be prepared to work, really hard to get there, and once you have, be prepared to work some more! Success isn't a given, it is a privilege you work hard to achieve and work even harder to maintain.

There are however, things you can do, to position yourself to be in a good place from the start ... Developing your 'Ideal Patient Profile' (see categories below) can really help focus your attention on the kind of patients you are looking to serve and how to attract them through your door.

I've found the best way to work through this exercise is with a page of A4 and a pen answering the following questions (be aware your ideal patient profile may well change over time so this exercise is worth repeating anytime you feel 'stuck' to make sure you are still targeting the right type of patient within your marketing strategy).

The Ideal Patient Profile

1   Are you planning on attracting men, women or both to your business? You could narrow this down even further if you see your niche serving the transsexual community or other sexual identities.

2   Who are you planning to market to? Really niche this down, how old is your ideal patient. What 'look' will they be aiming for?

3   What treatments and products are you aiming to use; are you aiming high-end, mid-range or budget?

4   What occupation would your ideal patient be?

5   What are their interests and hobbies?

6   Where do they spend their leisure time?

7   What social media do they use?

Answering the above questions (or others that you think are relevant) is vital for you to build your business, marketing plan and future developments. Ideally, spend some time writing a whole description about your ideal patient, really get to know them, feel into their life, understand them and really get to know your patient in-depth.

A good exercise to do is to write a story of your ideal patients' day. Where do they live? who lives with them? what do they like to eat? what do they like to wear? – everything! This will form the fundamentals of your advertising/marketing strategy, the more you can put into this the better, it is a substantial piece of work, take your time, think it through, make it real.

Where to invest

There will be no end of opportunities for you to spend money! Decide where you wish to focus your business development attentions on. Beware of investing broadly in a wide range of training, equipment or even advertising strategies which could distract you from your core focus. There is a temptation to grow rapidly in all kinds of different directions, especially if your business is in its infancy and you are trying to generate a speedy income. This can ultimately have the opposite effect whilst you dilute your services and try to be 'all things to all men' and do not really specialise in anything.

In many ways, it is wise to decide what your core products and services are and ensure you excel at these before branching out and developing into other areas. Be mindful that adding to your repertoire may increase your insurance premium, may require the purchase of additional equipment and certainly will include additional training fees.

Overall, play to your strengths. What are you good at and what do you enjoy doing? These are the things which will light you up and your patients will see this. Focusing on work which you are not passionate about is really setting yourself up to fail, your patients will sense your lack of enthusiasm and therefore won't be attracted in.

In this business, the decision a patient will make on whether or not to buy from you will hinge on the relationship you foster with them. You are your own 'unique selling point' so focusing on building relationships and being amazing at the stuff you love to do, will become your point of attraction. This is all about relationships, it is time to dig deep!

Personal Stories: Getting to know your patients, to foster a genuine care and interest in them is something I realised from very early on is vitally important. From the very beginning I have kept aid-memoirs in my patient records following each appointment to remind me of what is going on for my patients, in their lives, so I can pick things up with them at their next appointment. For example, I might note they are studying a particular course, or a major life event has just happened for them and what it was or if they were having a particularly bad or good day when I last saw them and why that was. There is absolutely nothing wrong in doing this and really helps develop these key relationships if you struggle remembering individual details about your patients. They will be touched you have remembered and asked about what is going on for them and you can be sure that you are not insensitive by being unaware of major events in their lives.

Occasionally, provided I know it will be well received, I will send a patient who is having a particularly rough time, some flowers or another token to let them know I'm thinking about them. The same applies for celebration, a bottle of fizz is always appreciated. I may gift a patient some skin care if they book in around their birthday and I always have small Christmas gifts for my patients who attend in December. None of this is contrived, it all comes from the heart and because I love to see my patients happy. This approach may resonate with you, or it may not, but whatever you do make sure it is authentically you. It is no good copying someone else's idea unless it is truly something you would have done already if you had thought of it earlier. Patients will see straight through you unless you are true to who you are. So, by all means, take my hints and tips. Use the exact same approach if it resonates with who you truly are, but if you relate to you patients in a different way, then do that. Only you can be you and your way will be just perfect for your patients.

5 WHY MINDSET MATTERS IN BUSINESS

Make no mistake, mindset is pivotal to your business success! On a personal note I can tell you that I spent a lot of time in my business doing all the things, I mean all of them ... with reasonable success. I was very focused on creating my successful business, I made sure I was up to date with all of the updates in the industry. I was attending conferences and investing in training. I had a treatment room to work from and a referral mechanism in place and was optimising this through other professionals I was linked to. I had policies and procedures established and was able to offer a

top-quality service, I had advertising mechanisms in place and targeted this within my local area.

All of this worked and contributed to helping me build my business however, I was very aware that business was 'steady' as opposed to 'flying'. Then I learned about mindset work, coaching, positivity, the law of attraction and the whole world changed! I kid you not, in the space of a month my business really took off and it is been flying ever since.

Mindset is a huge subject and weaves into the fabric of all your business development. Being in a good place mentally supports the development of your business in ways you cannot even begin to imagine unless you have experienced it. Giving yourself space to think and lifting the pressure we put on ourselves to succeed is so important, it is in this space that your ideas will begin to flow. In the next few chapters we will discuss various strategies to enable a positive mindset and then, how you can allow your ideas and therefore your business, to develop, grow and fly.

Pressure can be a very disabling emotion or feeling and is something we can all become victim to, at any stage, but especially in the early stages of running a business. The whole process of setting up and running a business can be exhausting, stressful and expensive. Then, once your venture is up and running in the world, we often apply a huge amount of pressure on ourselves to bring in business, repay any finances we owe, make the venture successful because we need to provide for our family, ourselves etc. All of this can cause enormous psychological pressure and I can absolutely guarantee that, when you feel this much pressure, bringing in new business will be at least twice as hard as when you feel less pressured and in a good place. There are various strategies and tools we can use to reduce this pressure and bring us to a state where we can allow our ideas and success to flow which are discussed in the next few chapters.

This knowledge is important, this is absolutely key to enabling an easier, happier way of working which in turn will create easy flow in your business and allow your success to happen, interested? Read on!

Personal Stories: Mindset is such a massive subject and can take on so many different meanings depending on the angle you are coming from. I have read extensively around business, self-development and how to succeed and have taken lots of valuable advice from many different books, podcasts, videos and courses. However, my biggest leaps have been made by being coached. It is an extremely valuable experience, if you find the right mentor. It is my experience that you really have to 'click' with a business coach in order to achieve the most from the experience.

I believe that this is because self-development is a very individual experience. What works for one person will hold no value for another. The same applies with any other self- development materials. There needs to be a synergy in terms of experiences, goals and demeanor for any individual to achieve the greatest outcomes, although, with effort, even without these things it is possible to take some valuable content; but the real gold is found where this formula exists.

For me, when I found my 'magic formula', I realised that I had been constantly trying to start in the middle. I focused on building my business, my clinical skills, my marketing knowledge etc. When I found the tools, which worked best for me, I realised that my starting point had been all wrong! Business development, for me, always must start with personal development and improvement. This is the formula I'm sharing with you in this book. It has been an incredible learning experience and I'm enjoying the ride; I do not expect the journey to ever end! However, had I realised earlier that starting with me, rather than starting with my business was the wiser move, I could potentially have saved myself years of exploration and heartache. I would have been more resilient, given off a better vibe and my whole approach to my life, as well as my business, would have been lifted sooner. So, if you feel there is always more to learn and can identify with my story, keep reading, join our 'Their Face, Your Business'

Facebook group and come and jump onboard with our masterminds. In my experience, your business is a reflection of you, so you need to be in great shape!

6 GETTING IN A GOOD PLACE

I can absolutely 100% totally and completely say that starting, developing and/or growing your business will be one long hard and negative slog if your head is not in the right place.

Bringing energy, enthusiasm and positivity to every part of your day and your soul is the single biggest influencing factor (in my experience) for developing your success.

It was my experience that, often, being positive and upbeat was something that I made an effort to be. At times this was draining and difficult and therefore felt inauthentic. This is not about 'putting a face on', this is about really feeling the good things, from the very core of your being and it is not something we always really know how to do.

In the current fast-paced, high pressured environment we live in, the joy can get sucked out of our lives and getting into a good place does not always feel like our normal natural state of being. The good news is that 'getting in a good place' is actually a skill which can be learned. The even better news is that once you have embraced this approach it is no longer inauthentic, or an effort, or draining. This is living in a state of joy, gratefulness, appreciation and happiness; this is when the magic happens, we feel better and even have more physical energy. So how do we do it and where do we start? It is remarkably simple really. It is a whole number of little things we do every day and you can start to feel good now, right now!

There are a number of ideas below, have a look through and pick the ones that speak to you (or invent some of your own). Make this a habit every day, practise feeling good, it will pay you back in all sorts of amazing ways.

Daily Feel-Good Habits

- First thing in a morning – wake up feeling good.
  - o Set your alarm to a song which makes you smile.
  - o Have a photograph next to your bed which always lifts your spirits.
  - o Spend a few minutes focusing on your breathing (many smart watches even have a relaxation app which helps you to do this).
  - o Put on some upbeat music and dance! Movement is a great way of lifting your mood.
  - o Create a gratitude list every day of the things which bring you joy, read this but feel into it too, this can be very powerful.
  - o Spend time outside – run, walk or just be. Feel the wind/rain/sun on your face appreciate the sensation of just being alive.
  - o Feeling antsy? Find something in the situation you are in to be grateful for.
  - o At the end of each day reflect on the people that you love – what is it you love about each of these people, do not forget to include what you love about yourself.

- o Make a list of things which light you up; this could be people who make you smile, experiences you have had, activities, emotions or even chocolate!
- o Exercise is a considerable mood booster so take the time to find something you enjoy be it a class, a team sport, a solo sport, walking, dancing whatever you love to do; find it, make time for it and watch it light you up!

Look again at your ideal patient profile. Be aware that you are likely to attract the kind of patients who resonate with you so whatever you expect from your patients you should emulate in your own day to day life.

What do you expect from your ideal patient that you have not built into your own way of being? What can you do to make that a part of how and who you are? Add this into your daily habits list and magnetise your ideal patients to your business.

Personal Stories: Of all the different strategies discussed in this book (and the many others besides) those which help me feel good now have been the most valuable. These tools are super simple but brilliantly effective, they impact your everyday approach to life, increase your resilience and have a positive impact on all your coping strategies.

The feel-good exercises changed my mindset around who I spend time with too. When you are in a good place and have the tools to keep there, it becomes more apparent when you spend time with those who are less positive and I found I really did not want that kind of negativity pulling me down. Lots of people going through these journeys of self-development discuss how they build a new circle of friends and associates who are of the same mindset. It does not mean you have to undertake any dramatic break ups or anything like that! Equally I absolutely want to be there for my friends and totally accept that we all have our ups and downs; even with all the feel-good methods going! What can be really useful though is spending time with people who stretch you, who encourage you to grow, who have a positive outlook and who are on a similar journey. I would really encourage you to find some groups for yourself both in real life and on-line. Do a simple search on 'aesthetics groups' in your area or even create your own. Look to other groups to join too, networking is always a good idea but also look to where your ideal patients may be. If you have shared interests with this group of people you may develop some fabulous friendships and wonderful patients all at the same time.

7 MAKE SOME SPACE

Once you are in the habit of feeling good now, or have started to bring some feel-good habits into your daily routine, you are going to need to make some space. Much like a box has a limited capacity, so does our environment and our head!

The physical process of clearing out the junk is utterly cathartic and I would massively encourage you to have a good ole clear out. This may not sound like a very business-like strategy (to be fair, it is unlikely a Masters in Business Administration would encourage you to have a mass declutter) but honestly, this is a process not to be skipped.

Trust me, now is the time to have a good sort out of your home, your workplace, your car, your handbag/man-bag whatever you can really. Clear out your wardrobe and donate or sell the clothes you no longer wear, get rid of the shoes you do not need, clear out your underwear drawer, get rid of the stuff that no longer serves you.

Do you have possessions that just sit there, clothes that no longer represent how you perceive yourself, clutter that just is not necessary? If so, then please just get rid; this is important, you are making space for the good stuff, things which do serve you, clothes which represent you, or the person you are growing into.

Have you got things you are 'saving for best'? Well get them out and enjoy using the 'good' dinnerware or your 'best' clothes, honestly, life is there to be enjoyed! Enjoy your 'good' possessions, you deserve that pleasure every day, not just on special occasions.

Make space to bring things which serve you into your life. Letting go is an amazing physical and emotional process, it may bring up some feelings of sadness or nostalgia and that is fine, but use this process to create positive energy.

The psychological benefits of this process are immense and a good physical declutter is brilliant for improving your environment, it will help you feel better and give you space to grow. The physical declutter is only half of the equation though, there is a second part to this exercise; the emotional clear out, this can take a bit more work, can bring up a number of emotions/feelings and can be a challenging process.

Declutter your time, if you are entering into a new venture you need to make the space for it and this does include time. Make time for your business to grow, make time to work both in your business and on your business. If your life was full before then what are you going to let go of? What activities which take up your time could be used more wisely elsewhere? Map out your day or week if it helps and see where your time could be better used and schedule your working time. If patients are not rolling through the door do not panic; use the time to develop your business, work on marketing plans, put yourself out there, make sure your policies and procedures are up-to-date, do some training etc. Use the time for your business even if it is a coffee out with your business partner/accountability partner to discuss ideas and developments. This is something I do on a regular basis, scheduled quality time with your team is essential for good communication, developing/deepening friendships, understanding if anyone is struggling with anything (personal or professional), offering peer support and growing creative ideas for business development.

Have an emotional clear out! We will talk more about this later but if there are emotional thoughts, feelings or circumstances which are holding you back it is time to put these down. Emotional baggage will drag you down and give you a negative focus; this will not serve you or your business and not only that, it will cause you to self-sabotage yourself and your business. There are a whole variety of strategies for doing this but at this stage recognising what thoughts and feelings are holding you back or are in your way is a really good start. From there we can work on how to move more positively forward.

Personal Stories: I Genuinely did not have a clue how powerful this exercise is until I gave it a go! It was tough letting so of some 'stuff' that was just taking up space but had some sentimental value but the sense of freedom, clarity and release afterwards was totally worth it! I felt liberated by getting rid of some of my old possessions and bringing items which I had kept 'for best' and never really used. Not only is this a great practical exercise in creating space for some good stuff, but it also increased my sense of self-worth.

It may sound a bit stupid but by allowing myself to wear my 'best' clothes, use my 'best' crockery and getting rid of all the old stuff so really, there was no option to go back and use the items which were a bit 'past their best'. It made me value myself more which had a knock-on effect into other areas of my life including my business. I learned that my time is valuable and I started actively enforcing my 'booking fee' policy with my patients; something I had always had, but not always adhered to. I realised that my time is valuable and that, by taking a booking fee, I was highlighting to myself and to my patients, that my time is precious and that patients booking and not turning up (trust me, they will if you do not take a booking fee) is not respecting my own value.

Having a physical declutter is a brilliant exercise ahead of the psychological declutter too. If I am honest, I was a little afraid of the 'letting things go' aspect of the psychological clear out. I was worried that this exercise would bring things up I did not want to think about and that the process of forgiveness might be too painful or too emotional for me to manage. The thing is, I really did not understand initially, what this process was all about.

Forgiveness / letting stuff go / creating psychological

space is all about being kind to yourself. It is a process of forgiving yourself for holding onto things for too long and cause you to dwell on things which bring you down rather than lift you up. It is actually a beautiful act of self-care which is freeing, liberating and uplifting. It re-directs your energies from a negative flow to a positive flow and that is utter magic.

You may have heard of people being 'in-flow'. This happens when you are happy, relaxed, positive, buoyed up rather than weighed down; everything just seems to effortlessly fall into place. The process of having a good old clear out (on a physical and emotional level) really enables this flow to kick in. I recommend you give it a go, pop onto the 'Their Face, Your Business' Facebook page and let me know how you get on.

8 PAY ATTENTION

Where your focus goes, energy flows! This is such a
true saying but in order to make this work for you, it is
not just about where you focus, it is how you focus. Let
me give you an example:

There are 2 people, both trying to lose a little weight
and tone up, let us call them Bill and Jeff ...

Bill puts himself on a diet restricting his calorie intake
and spends a lot of time thinking about what he cannot
eat. He keeps a food diary and tells people about what
is restricted from his diet. He joins the gym, but this is
not really his favourite activity so he spends time
thinking about having to go and do this activity he does
not enjoy.

Jeff thinks about taking control of his nutrition, his focus is on the exciting new foods he is going to incorporate into his diet. He keeps a food diary and looks forward to trying new recipes. Jeff finds an activity he enjoys (running/walking/dancing etc) and looks forward to his regular exercise sessions. He pays attention every day to how he looks and feels focused on how positive he is feeling celebrating every little win he notices on the journey.

So, which of these two fellas do we think will do best to trim and tone up? They are both focused on their desired outcome, both in their own eyes working hard but, do you agree, that Bill really is setting himself up to fail? His full attention is on what he is giving up or having to do as a 'chore' rather than for pleasure. Jeff is focused on his amazing new diet and activities he enjoys. Both gents may achieve their end goal but Jeff is definitely going to enjoy the process far more and is likely to achieve sustainable results and a real lifestyle change. Bill will resent the whole process and the moment he reaches his target is likely to give up completely and be back to square one within a month.

Where the goal is associated with a positive focus, you are much more likely to achieve positive, long-term results than when you have a negative perspective.

Applying this within a business context relies on the same principles. Keeping the focus positive will pay huge dividends; celebrate every little win no matter how small. I have lost count of how many practitioners have said 'I went into aesthetics, but it just didn't work for me'. Here's the thing, it doesn't 'just' work for anyone. Any business requires commitment, time, investment and damned hard work but you will totally get out what you put in. Therefore, where you are focusing really, really matters. It matters because your focus affects the vibe you emit and that in turn radiates out towards your patients. If you have a positive, upbeat, enthusiastic, passionate approach to your business, your energy will be high and this will draw patients towards you. Approach your business from the perspective of 'it is really, really difficult, patient's do not come to me, I am not confident' etc then this is exactly what you will attract; you will find the work tough, patients will pick up on your negativity and they will not book in with you.

Of course, it is very easy to write this, however, changing to a positive mindset is not something you can just 'put on'; you will be inauthentic if you are not feeling it and this will communicate itself to your patients. There are many tools and techniques you can use to move you into a better place, build your positivity and influence your overall approach to business and life in general.

In my experience, working on focus is an absolute game changer. We are going to spend time further on in the book looking at exercises, routines and techniques which can help you move into a better place in order to take your business forward in a positive and proactive way. Also take a look at the 'recommended reading list' at the back of this book for other authors who delve into this subject on a much deeper level. For now, start to develop an awareness of your attitude and approach to life. Be mindful of the vibes you are emitting and how you come across to other people. Having this kind of self-awareness will be really helpful as we bring in techniques to lift you into a good place (if you are not already) later on in the book.

Personal Stories: Over the last few years one of the things I have learned more about and got really quite good at is managing money. I have not always been the greatest at this though! It took a fair bit of reading for me to figure out why, and guess what ... it is really not rocket science! I realised the reason for my perception of lack of money (because that is what I worried about the most) was because I really was not paying enough attention to the subject. As a youngster (way before the age of the internet) I had been fabulous at keeping a cash book, I kept every receipt, balanced my statement at the end of the month and know exactly, to the penny what was coming in and going out. I never fully took my eye off the ball but with more accessible ways to monitor incomings and outgoings and with a larger income I had become complacent. I never got into any financial trouble, but there were times when I realised things were a little tight and I had not seen it coming (I am talking on a personal level here, on a business level I have always been very aware of the bank balance)! So, what did I do and what difference did it make? The short answer is, I started to pay attention. I now check all of my bank accounts every day. I note the incomings and outgoings and query anything which does not look familiar. Not only this I have started to pay attention and celebrate everything which comes my way. This may not be cash, but if someone is kind enough to buy me a coffee, or I find a 20 pence in the street, or I get a (useful) money off coupon I am so grateful and celebrate all the little wins (sometimes it is only an 'internal happy dance') but it is important.

Being grateful and celebrating all the little wins, be it money related, or kindness or anything else, opens you up to receiving. It is my experience that the more you appreciate the good things, by being grateful and by celebrating, the more you will receive. The same applies to anything, whether you are wanting to be more in control of your finances (and have more money) to getting fit, losing weight ... whatever your goal is, give it some attention. Set your goal and monitor it daily, celebrate all the successes, be open to accepting more. Cultivate that excited feeling you get in your stomach when good things are on their way (remember how you felt as a child on Christmas Eve or your birthday) and try to feel that every time something wonderful comes your way, no matter how big or small.

The first time I was introduced to these concepts was a real eye-opener for me. By closely mapping my incomings and outgoings and assigning a monetary value to 'stuff' I received or was gifted, I began to really appreciate the extent of abundance I was receiving. I really had no idea how lucky I was and often how that related to kindness to me from other people. I have repeated this exercise on a number of occasions, sometimes on my own and at times as part of a group.

The group exercises are really powerful and bring a bigger focus to the whole experience. By sharing wins or stories about what we have each received, it made us all more open to receiving and very appreciative of everything which came our way. When you are open to receiving, you are much likely to receive more, in all kinds of ways. It may be financial, but there are also lots of other good things which may come your way too.

Equally, when you give more, you will also notice that an abundance of good things often come your way in return. Goodwill is priceless, showing you care – invaluable. The positive impact of giving can be noticed in all areas of your life, family, personal, business … everywhere! It is an uplifting and beautiful experience to be generous with others be it with your time, a gift, money; whatever is needed at the time and will pay you back fabulously!

To get you kickstarted with this, I challenge you, for a month, to keep a record of everything you receive in fine detail. You can use the notes app on your phone but there are a couple of really good apps out there for this too. Download 'The Secret – Finance' app, or the 'Lucky Bitch' app and record everything which comes your way. It may be your salary but if someone does buy you a coffee, put a monetary value too it and log in down. Found some money? Log it down. Received a gift? Assign a monetary value and log it down. At the end of the month add up everything you have received and take a look at your actual income – you may well be very surprised! Join in on the 'Their face, your business' Facebook group and let me know how you get on.

9 GET CLEAR ON YOUR DIRECTION OF TRAVEL

This is kind of a big one! What are you aiming for? What kind of business are you looking to develop and how can you get there?

A really good way of looking at this is through reverse engineering; what is your overall business goal? This could relate to all kind of things but as an example, are you looking to develop into a bigger organisation, are you looking to expand your portfolio, are you looking to recruit more staff or do more treatments? Consider what your ideal scenario will look like and then start the reverse engineering to see what you need to do to make this happen. For example, if your goal is to generate an income of £10,000 per month, what kind of treatments do you need to be doing to achieve this within the time you have available? How many of them per month and how much time will this take? Do you need to develop packages or a stronger treatment planning regime? This is a really useful exercise to do in order to really understand what is achievable for you. If, for example, you have 8 hours clinical time available per week and average £250 per treatment, the absolute maximum you are likely to be able to make financially is roughly £104,000 (gross per year). If however, your average treatment had a higher price point you may easily push beyond this point ... of course the same applies if you are doing generally cheaper treatments and the finances would be similarly reduced.

The benefit of doing this exercise really helps you to position yourself in the market. It provides you with some cold hard facts to help you understand where you are, where you want to go and what capacity you have to achieve that ... it helps you build a plan and value your own worth.

Equally, remember that these numbers may look big however they are gross, not net. Factor in all your additional expenses as discussed earlier to really understand what this kind of income means in real terms.

The ideal patient work discussed earlier, also feeds directly into this section so if you are not completely clear on this, now would be a good time to go back and look again at who you are marketing to. What are your standards in terms of who you will treat, who you won't treat and who you are targeting?

What are your income goals? Are they achievable and what do you need to change to make them achievable if they're not?

What training/equipment/knowledge do you need to progress in your chosen direction?

Do you need support to do this? Do you need to look to other people with specific skills to take over work which has now become time consuming and distracting you from your core skills or to bring new skills and custom into your business? This kind of delegation often relates to administrative tasks, IT, accountancy or anything which is not within your core skill set.

Be aware of what is popular within the industry at the moment and what you need to do to move with the times and remain current. Are the new developments/fashions not something your ideal patient will want and therefore you can give this one a miss? There is a huge trend in many different lip techniques for the various current fashion looks at the moment. Does this require training investment on your part to gain competency or is this something you can sit out?

On a very practical note beware of 'shiny object syndrome'. Particularly when you are new in the industry there is huge temptation (and pressure) to buy the newest gadget, do the latest training, invest, invest, invest. We all want to succeed right? We all want to be the best we can be and develop a thriving business. So, when we see some amazing training being advertised, or a 'miracle working' machine, or a conference we just 'have' to attend, it is so very tempting to go all in. There is nothing wrong with that, investing in your business is essential whatever stage you are at however people are employed to sell you these things, it is their job to convince you that you just cannot live without 'x' or 'y' and sometimes you actually can.

Do your homework, ask around, canvass the forums, read reviews and generally make sure you are fully informed before you make any firm decision and investment. Goods with large outlays (machinery etc) should be available to you for a trial period before you make a commitment to buy; but you may have to ask for this, after all who is going to turn down an up-front sale? Pop onto the 'Their Face, Your Business' Facebook page if you have doubts, need pointers, help or impartial advice and do not be pressured into a 'same day' sale etc. If people really want your business they will help and support you with your buying decision. If they are not prepared to do that then are you really prepared to buy from them?

Personal Stories: It was through a personal coaching call with one of Daniel Priestley's team that the whole reverse engineering thing hit home for me. I knew what I wanted to make financially. Equally I knew what kind of treatments were my popular ones and the time I had available to do them. What I had not done was the maths! During this particular call we worked backwards from my desired financial goal to figure out exactly what my capacity needed to be in order to reach that. From this exercise, it became clear that in order to reach my own goals I needed to re-think my clinical business model including who I was marketing too and the products and packages on my menu.

This was a lightbulb moment for me (and probably sounds very obvious to many of you)! It really made me stop and consider my way forward and it is a methodology I have used ever since. It has also reinforced to me the importance of having clear goals and a plan regarding how to achieve them.

Equally, deciding what my goals are, at times, has been a struggle. I cannot claim to have found the 'magic formula' for clarifying where I am headed. What I have learned is that, in times of confusion, it is important to take a breather, relax, exercise and allow my mind to settle. This is when my inspirations shows up the most, the ideas flow and the goals emerge. My best advice to you, if your unclear about your direction of travel is to give yourself time, a chance to think, reflect and receive the inspiration which will appear if you are not in a place of panic, worry or distress. The morale of the story … chill out and the answers will appear!

10 MARKETING

There are many, many facets to this, it is a whole science in itself but it is really worth spending the time to master this. Visibility is key, you cannot expect people to come to you for treatment if they cannot find you.

The good news is that getting visible really is not too hard. These days we are looking largely to the internet for our information so if you are visible there, you have an excellent starting point. A website is ideal but if this is not something you want to invest in just yet, then social media is the way forward. Even if you do have a website, social media is still the way forward. It is just the way the world works these days so make sure you have a presence online and that you can easily be found on Google. There are tonnes of YouTube video's available which can advise you about this, just search 'google optimisation'. There is no right and wrong for the best social media platform to use either; many people use several. My best advice would be to go back to your ideal patient work and think about which platform they would use and focus on that. For me, it is largely Facebook. A slightly younger demographic may be more in tune with Instagram. Focus on what suits you and your patients best.

There are lots of different tools, forums, techniques and approaches to marketing but the holy grail you need to remember throughout is that your prospective patients need to feel they like, know and trust you before they are likely to take that leap and book an appointment.

LIKE: The news is not great here – not everyone is going to like you! Honestly, you can be the most likeable, lovely person in the world and someone will still find something to complain about. The fact remains though, you do not need everyone to like you; you need your ideal patient to like you and seeing as your ideal patient is the kind of person you choose to attract to your business, there is a good chance you will share some of the same standards, ethics and values. This makes things so much easier. It is easy to like people with whom you have things in common and shared principles. Do not take it personally when people do not like you, after all we cannot all like everyone and you probably do not want people who you do not really connect with to be one of your patients anyway.

Again, the ideal patient work is vital here. You need to be very clear on the kind of patient you want to serve in order to make yourself known and liked by them. This leads us on nicely to the next section ....

KNOW: These days people really do their homework. Before they even consider visiting your business, they have done a Google search, Facebook stalk and checked you out on LinkedIn! The world really is online these days so you need to get your social media ducks in a row. This is so easy to say but often, particularly for health professionals who often shy away from the limelight, it is much, much harder to do. I can relate! For years I 'hid' behind a social media profile that did not state my full name. Even when I got past that, I spent time hiding behind my business name but here is the thing, your business name is not you. People want to get to know a person, not a business. Aesthetics is personal. Potential patients want to interact with someone visible, someone real and someone who they can get an authentic feel for so they can decide whether you are their kind of person way before they ever meet you.

So, how can you do this? The short answer is, you need to put yourself out there! You need to be visible and known both online and in real life. People need to see you! One of the simplest (but often scary) ways of doing this is via livestream video; Insta, Facebook, YouTube – whatever you feel most comfortable with really, but I would absolutely encourage you to do this. It does not need to be insanely professional (although if you have a professional film crew kicking around, feel free!) Many livestreams are very informal but they get to showcase the real you. I know some people who will do a live for 2 hours and others who will do 2 minutes, it really does not matter (in all honesty 2 hours is far too long for my attention span, more than 30 mins and I am all done!) What matters is what you are putting across …. and it can literally be anything. I would encourage you to consider discussing issues which crop up repeatedly for your patients. Failing that, do a little tour of your treatment room, take us through your cleaning routine, take us through your skincare routine, tell us about your day, anything really so your prospective patients can learn about you.

If you are stuck for ideas, take a look at www.answerthepublic.com it is great for giving you all sorts of ideas for questions you can answer, just type in a few key words and off you go.

Other ways of getting to know your potential patients is to actually meet people in real life. It almost feels like a dying artform these days but there is no real substitute for actual interaction. Again, go back to your ideal patient profile. Where will this person hang out? What are their interests? Where are you likely to come across them (and I do not mean in some weird stalker kind of way)? Just consider what interests you are likely to have in common and where that will place you. You can do this exercise virtually as well as geographically as there are groups for literally everything on social media and many are linked with physical meet ups. Consider networking events, sports clubs, stamp collecting, train spotting – whatever floats your boat really but engage, connect, give people the opportunity to get to know you (not your business). Once people know you and you have taken a genuine interest in them, when what you do for a living comes up in conversation, if they are interested, they may well think of you. It is also a great way of growing your circle and seeing what you can offer and support others with. Go into this with the right approach, this is not about selling, this is about building relationships and seeing how that develops.

You may make some fabulous friends who will never be patients, but your life will be richer for knowing these wonderful people and for that you will be grateful for.

TRUST: This will follow naturally if people get to like and know you first however, there are things which can help. Often, in order to trust you, prospective patients may seek the opinion of others. Here is an ideal opportunity for you to provide them with the information they are looking for. Reviews, recommendations and testimonials are all excellent ways of building trust with those you are reaching out to. Equally, these real-life connections you have built are the same wonderful people who (even if they have not had treatments with you) can speak knowledgeably about you, tell people what you are like and recommend you to others who may book in for treatments.

It can be a challenge in Aesthetics, however, to get recommendations and reviews etc. Many patients really do not want to publicly acknowledge they have had treatments which really limits your potential for direct reviews. There are ways around this; if patient's compliment you privately, you can anonymise their compliment and post this on your social media pages.

You can story-tell on your livestreams about the really good experiences you have had in your clinic; your patient's reaction, experience, how you supported them etc.

Another way is to reach out to people via your social media channels. Post engaging items – anything from patient stories, questions, inspirational quotes, cute puppy pictures (!) whatever drives engagement and allows you to connect. Many people are 'silent watchers' and will be looking at your posts for a long, long time before they will consider contributing. These people will see your engagement, your contributions and how you manage people, it is important that you are aware that there can be a lot of people doing this so what you put and how you manage your posts really matters.

Something we all come up against at some point are the trolls. Again, these people watch in the wings. They may be friends or relatives of people who are engaging with you and they often have strong views about Aesthetics which they relay onto your page, or to anyone who will listen. These comments are often derogatory, opinionated and aggressive. They can be quite upsetting to read particularly when it feels like someone is criticising your hard work. Be assured, these posts provide you with a golden opportunity, not particularly to engage with the trolls, but to answer them, in a way which can be beneficial for your business.

Not too long ago I had someone posting on my business page that they could not understand why anyone would have such treatments when they could donate the money to charity and do good with it instead. Although I was a little upset initially to have received a negative comment, I was also very grateful for the engagement (Facebook does not care what the comments say, it is all engagement to them and will positively affect your visibility). My response was to thank the person who contributed for their opinion and stated that it is an interesting debate with a wide range of opinions. I stated that many of my patients do amazing charitable work and often they are confident doing this because of the treatments they have had which have given them their 'sparkle' back, increased their confidence and energy which in turn knocks on positively to the amazing things they achieve. I closed by thanking the contributor again, stating that it is always good to have the conversation and I would be happy to answer any further questions they may have. I did not hear from that person again, but I did get some new enquiries from other people. That post may or may not have been a catalyst for others to get in touch. Either way I was able to take something positive rather than negative from the experience. I came away feeling good about my response and have built on the holy grail of 'like, know and trust' for those observing who did not already know me.

Spread your net wide! There are so, so many platforms out there where we can be visible, it can be totally overwhelming but pick the ones which work for you and use them to your best advantage. My current top favourites are; Facebook, Twitter, Instagram and YouTube. There are some fabulous apps which allow you to schedule and publish posts to all of these simultaneously (I like RIPL but there are others). Ideally your content should vary on each platform but we do not always have the time, patience or inclination to work that way. Equally, you may well meet different types of people on the different forums. I post to Instagram with very similar content to that which I post on Facebook. Over the years I have had many, many patients find me on Facebook and yet not one has contacted me via Instagram or twitter. For me, my ideal patient base is a Facebook user which works well because that is what I know and can manage best. I have friends in the business, who serve a slightly younger demographic to the one I do, who find Instagram to be far more effective for them; but then that is their platform of choice too. It all comes back down to who your ideal patient is and where they spend their time. Take a look, do your research on this and you will get it right.

Besides your own social media profiles, raise the visibility of your business with a Facebook business page and a linked group. Groups (at the moment) are a great way of increasing your reach on social media. A few rules apply: make sure your members are engaging, it is much better to have a small group with lots of active and engaged members, than a group of hundreds of people who do not really interact at all. Facebook algo-rhythms monitor engagement and if you have high engagement, will show your group to other people who may be interested in what you are doing. Obviously, if you have great content but little engagement, Facebook will not widely show your content in news feeds or 'other groups you may be interested in' so it is worth monitoring your groups performance and ensuring your engagement remains high.

Blogging is also a fabulous way of sharing information, providing education, updating people on your developments and can provide so much content which can be used in a variety of forms. You can take elements from a blog post to compose social media posts, use the content in related live streams and publish across all your platforms. It is worthwhile publishing at least one blog post a month and using material from this to support all of your other material for the month.

Get published! Having reports, studies and articles in peer reviewed publications will increase your credibility within the industry, raise your profile and potentially create a number of different opportunities for you. Information on how to do this is usually published within each journal, the peer review process usually means that you will be asked to undertake some changes or amendments to your original piece, do not be discouraged by this, it is totally normal (and expected) for this to happen and it is totally worth the work.

Finally, be very, very clear on the advertising standards. The Advertising Standards Agency have tightened up again and introduced even more stringent monitoring for 2020. Have a good read (link below) and do not fall foul of the rules.

https://www.asa.org.uk/uploads/assets/a8fa05da-
b3ee-4528-82095e7bba2a3e5c/Enforcement-Notice-
Advertising-Botox-and-other-botulinum-toxin-
injecti.pdf?fbclid=IwAR3mTANRYQGtPJ4N-
l2eMzTySL_Dke63s1r86noOrX_MsoZ9g8Tu0jm7n-E

Personal Stories: So, I was the absolute worst at this!
Hiding was my thing. I wanted a business, I wanted to
be successful but I did not want to put myself out there!
It is absolutely remarkable (on reflection) that I did as
well as I did, given how invisible I made myself. It took
me a long time to get over myself and just get on with it
and that was a long process. I had so many blocks;
worries about what other people would think, fear of
being rejected, loathed seeing pictures or videos of
myself, feeling it was 'wrong' to put myself forward –
the full gambit of 'what not to do's' really! It has taken
years to feel good enough about myself to just not care
too much about what other people think. It really
would not have taken anywhere near this long if I had
known and practised the feel-good strategies in this
book sooner!

So, if you are scared, like I was (and still am at times if I
am honest) about taking that big scary step out there,
peering over the parapet and allowing yourself to be

seen, I suggest you just start small, take baby steps and gain confidence that the world really will not stop spinning and nothing else too scary will happen, before slowly opening up to the process.

Here is what I did:

- The occasional personal social media post about fun or interesting activities I was doing.
- The occasional photograph of myself, maybe in clinic, maybe out socially; this was a huge and scary step for me but after a few posts of myself, when no-one was unkind, the sky did not fall in etc. I began to lose my feelings of self-consciousness and my confidence began to grow.
- I had been told many, many times that live videos on the platform of my choice was the way to go ... but I was not quite ready to jump straight to the live video. Instead I started by posting videos I had pre-recorded (only on my phone, nothing very professional!) and built my confidence that way. It was a good 'step up' as I could watch the video back before I posted it and be reasonably happy that I had not messed up too much!
- Eventually I braved a live stream video! This was a big step but not so terrifying after doing a few pre-recorded versions first.

- These days I do at least one live in all of my groups every week. I have video teachings which are accessed by students all over the world. I speak at conferences, present at group meetings, do radio interviews, engage in national video interviews in a number of forums all in addition to my one to one training and mentoring sessions.

From someone who would shy away from any one of the above situations I am now in a place where I actively enjoy doing these things. I am still 'me', definitely not an attention seeker by nature. However, I recognised what I needed to do to 'step-up' to support my business, to be the face of my business who my patients can get to 'like, know and trust'. In putting myself at the forefront of my

business, I was able to develop positive relationships, and make my business feel a lot more personal to my patients. In doing this, I found confidence, enjoyment and reward throughout the process. If you are in a similar place to where I was a few years ago, challenge yourself to take the first few scary steps. If it feels uncomfortable, just remind yourself that these are normal growing pains. Welcome these feelings, it shows you are growing and are on the right path. The rewards will come!

11 PRACTICALITIES

When it comes to running a business on a practical day-to-day level, there is so much to do. It really is not possible for one person to do it all well. It is highly unlikely that anyone is brilliantly skilled in every aspect of running their business, so below are my top tips for picking your way through the practicalities of being a business owner and how to navigate the perils!

Play to your strengths: If you are a clinical person, I would really expect your strengths to be in the clinical side of the business. You may not be the best website developer or accountant but it really does not matter if you are a brilliant injector who patients connect with. Excel at what you are good at and recognise what you are not so good at.

Automate: Automate everything you can! This will save you so much time and money you would not believe! There is plenty you can automate. Get a great booking system which will automatically send confirmations, reminders etc to your patients. Use Google or Siri or whoever you like to keep track of what pharmacy orders you need to submit or what stock items you are running out of. If there is anything else you can automate, do that too! There really is enough to manage on a daily basis, make life as easy for yourself as you can.

Delegate: For those things you cannot do yourself (either due to skills or time) and you cannot automate, delegation is the way forward. From the very, very first day my business was alive, I have had an accountant. This poor chap has looked after me so well, I have the most amazing spreadsheet which keeps me right on track, thanks to him. He tolerates my year-end panics with a degree of 'laid-back' I will never achieve and yet everything happens when it should and most importantly, stacks up!

I never pretended that accountancy would ever be something I would excel at, I recognised this and made arrangements to engage help. For me it really is an investment, it is saving me time, stress and worry – totally worth it! Equally, I was never, ever in a million years going to be able to build myself an amazing professional website but I needed one. Once again, delegation was the way forward for this and I have a wonderful website now, properly built and functioning with very little stress to me.

As my business has grown, so have the associated daily tasks. To manage this my team has also grown and these days I have a wonderful vPA who takes care of most of the business administration. This is an absolute god-send for me and leaves me free to do work on the business and in the business whilst she takes care of keeping the wheels turning.

Invest: When you have exhausted the Automate and Delegate options and you still have skills gaps, then investment is required. Updating clinically is vital in this industry, being prepared to manage complications etc is essential. Do not be afraid to invest. My second biggest spend every year is on training and it pays dividends. When you need expert advice, training or support in any area of your business, investment is required. Plan this in to your annual financial projections and particularly in the early days, expect that training is where any profit you do make will go.

Personal Experience: Like many solo practitioners, in the early days, almost everything I was capable of doing, I did. Only the website and accountancy were outsourced (I have always been totally aware of my limitations)! I do not regret this at all and if I was starting again now, I would probably do the same again. There is plenty you can automate though (probably much more than I am actually aware of) and much of it can be cost free.

For example:

- A good booking system will automatically send your patients text and email reminders pre appointment.

- A few years ago, I found an app on my android phone which allowed SMS messages to be scheduled and sent in advance and for some time this was a fabulous way of ensuring my patients were contacted in a timely way after their treatment to see how they were getting on. Sadly, I lost this facility when I updated my phone but I am sure there is a way to do this, I am just not sure how! I am lucky enough that my vPA takes care of this for me these days so I do not really need to learn, however I would recommend it if you are still at the stage of keeping all the balls in the air yourself. I can put you in touch with people who can help with this if you need!

- Although I have a wonderful accountant, I also have an amazing spreadsheet too! This keeps all of my finances in order so we both know where we are at. There is plenty of accountancy apps and software out there to automate as much of this process as possible for you and again, I can put you in touch with a specialist Aesthetics Accountant if you would like. Just reach out on the 'Their Face, Your Business', Facebook group.

- I use the reminders and notes apps on my phone for everything. Whilst this does not automate things for you, it is fabulous for keeping you in check. I have a reminder each week to check my stock and pharmacy requirements and put in any requests I need for the week ahead. I use it to remind me to check my finances. My notes contain my goals and task list. They are such simple tools but really help with organisation and simply getting things done.

12 DEVELOPING A WINNING MINDSET

You can have all the strategies, goals and targets in the world, do not get me wrong, all that work is really valuable and necessary, but, without the right mindset you will always feel the struggle.

Developing your mindset is about really understanding what is going on inside your head and how this has a direct impact on your environment, how people treat you and your ability to succeed. It is an absolute game-changer in business, it is the difference between plodding and flying and the good news is that it is all within your control and completely within your reach.

Some aspects we have already discussed or touched on

however, in the next few chapters we are going to look at specific tools and exercises you can develop and make part of your daily routine.

Mindset is a bit of an all or nothing deal; you cannot dabble at this, it does not work. You really do need to be all-in to see the benefits. It is the difference (for those of you who watch some of the reality talent shows like Strictly Come Dancing), between the celebrity who feels a bit daft so does not really throw themselves into the experience, looks uncomfortable, wooden and gets voted off in the first round, and the celebrity who embraces the whole experience and gives it everything they have. They are the ones who yield the benefit (even if they have 2 left feet) because they are totally onboard with the whole experience and throw themselves at it.

Do not get me wrong, I am the ultimate pragmatist and not at all 'woo-woo' in my thinking. I believe there has to be rational and logical explanations to any approach which makes good sense for me, but, even with my pragmatist head on, I cannot deny that self-development, particularly in the area of mindset, absolutely turned my business from doing okay (sometimes even really well), to being totally on fire.

When I got my head around developing an abundant mindset, my income generation ability skyrocketed and there was a phenomenal positive change within my business as a whole.

So, how to get started? Well, like it or not, this work is hugely based on your feelings. Therefore, you need to take control, understand why you are feeling the way you are and learn to focus in the right direction. It is not hard, but you really need to mean this, to feel it in your bones. Paying lip service to any of the upcoming tools will not serve you and will set you up to fail. So, for a few weeks, indulge me. Try these tools out with your heart, mind and soul. Feel them to the fibre of your being. They will have a significant impact on so many areas of your life you will not believe, including in your business.

Gratitude: as a society we are great at criticism, we love to highlight the flaws of others and as Brits (sorry guys!) we do this particularly well.

The thing is, negativity and criticism is toxic, the better we get at it, the more toxic it becomes – it is time to stop!

Gratitude is an artform and learning it is so much more than making a list. It is a state of mind which it is so important to live in and cultivate. We all know it is better for our mental health to focus on the positives, we all know it is better for our relationships (work, friends, life partner) when we are not constantly critical or criticised, we all respond far better to appreciation than negativity – we know this and yet embedding the principles into every aspect of life does not come easily. It takes dedication, a determination to do better, to be better and an appreciation that this is a huge, deep subject and much more complex than many people appreciate.

So, how do we develop 'an attitude of gratitude' and why would you want to? Well, let us answer the 'why' first. By living in a gratitude mindset, we actually make life so much easier for ourselves. We rid ourselves of negative energy, if you develop this skill, you will find you really do not have the desire to engage in negative conversations (with yourself or with others) about other people or situations. Your whole approach will change to something far more positive, energised and constructive. This has a direct knock-on effect on every single aspect of your life, including your business. It impacts on the energy you emit and therefore the vibes your patients will pick up from you. As we have discussed already, the way others perceive you will influence whether or not they will want to work with you. Generally speaking, someone who is positive, energised and living in gratitude will emit a much more attractive energy than someone who is negative, critical and complaining. Your patients (actually, everyone around you) will pick up on your attitude or your energy and if that is positive, they will want to spend time with you, book your treatments, come for consultations and increase your business.

There are a number of tools you can use to embed this approach in your day to day life. I challenge you to try at least one of them every day for a month and then reflect on the impact this has had at the end of the month and which areas of your life have been positively impacted by this.

The Gratitude Tools

1   Spend time each day, first thing is great if you can, to really think about what you are grateful for in your life. This needs to go deeper than a list, you totally need to feel

into this. If by considering a few points you are grateful for it feels too much of a list and you are not really feeling it, then just choose one. Pick one that means the most to you and spend 5 minutes or so really thinking into your one thing, really feel into why you are grateful for this, make it emotional and hold onto that feeling through the day.

2   Celebrate everything! Every enquiry, every phone call, every appointment, absolutely everything. Do a little happy dance when the phone rings (even if it is a cold calling sales person), celebrate every booking, every booking fee in your bank account as well as everything that goes out! Be grateful that you have bills to pay, it means you have a business you are responsible for! Find something to celebrate about everything. Managing a complaint? Take a good look at what you can learn from the experience and be grateful for that.

3   Find the positives in the irritating! This can be challenging, but is a very powerful thing to do. It is different for everyone but some examples would be:

a.   Irritated that a patient cancelled at late notice -> grateful for the additional time you have to work on your business.

b. Irritated that the kids are ignoring you -
    > grateful to have them and to be
    spending time with them (but yes, they
    do still need to listen!)
c. Irritated that someone did not do a job
    to the standard you would have liked ->
    grateful that they tried.

I am sure there are thousands of examples
we can all bring to the table, but you get
the idea. It does not mean that you ignore
what is going wrong, however, if you can
find something to appreciate in the
situation, there is a very good chance that
you will manage it better and get your point
across in a much more positive and
effective way.

Developing this approach can really lift your mood,
outlook and approach, it is often the littlest things
which can have a huge impact. I remember leaving
work after a really horrendous NHS shift, I felt terrible;
sad, angry and upset. As I walked outside, I felt the sun
on my face, I took some deep breaths and really
appreciated the warm sun, the beautiful plants and
trees. It was a very calming experience and helped to
moderate the negative feelings I was experiencing; it
does not mean you do not acknowledge the negatives

(we all have them and it would be wrong to try and pretend they are not there). It just means we can use strategies around gratefulness to limit the damage the negative emotions do and give us a positive anchor – we all need that.

Forgiveness: Another absolute must, if you are working on your mindset is to learn forgiveness. This falls into so many categories and is such a powerful tool.

We spoke earlier about making space and forgiveness is a huge part of that. Our minds do have a limit on the capacity of emotion we can hold and if we are hanging onto bitterness, resentment, anger or any other negative emotions we are limiting the space for the 'good' emotions to hang out in.

This is not about massive gestures towards others (although it can be if you feel the need). This is about recognising what we have held onto for too long which is eating us up (but probably having no effect on the person or situation which caused the emotional upset in the first place). The process of forgiveness in this instance is about self-acceptance and love. It is about identifying the negatives within us and making a conscious decision to let this stuff go, put it down and move on without it, thereby creating space for happiness, positivity and gratitude to come into your heart and mind and make their home there.

People do this in different ways. Some like to write down all the things which are causing them distress and go through the process of burning the paper it is written on, as a way of symbolising the 'letting go'. Others prefer to talk it out, some may pray, I often like to go for a run. Whatever works for you is what matters. We are aiming for the end result, how you get there, in many respects is irrelevant. What matters is the process of:

- Recognition of the negatives taking up space in your mind.

- A process of forgiveness or 'letting go'.

- Creating space for the good stuff to come in.

This is likely to be an ongoing process, in fact none of the strategies in this book are a one-time only fix. It is easy to fall back into negative thinking or hold onto grudges if that has been our default for a long time. The skill is to recognise what you are doing and take the necessary remedial action.

It is a great idea to do a 'psychological self-check' each day, notice your thoughts, what are you ruminating on and do you need to let it go? Give it a try each day for a week (set a reminder on your phone so you have a schedule to do this). See how you feel afterwards and what impact your new approach has on you and those around you, you may be amazed!

Personal Experience: All I can say here is 'total gamechanger'! Several years ago, I was doing okay. I had an established business; I had a reasonable number of patients booked in but could not shake the feeling that I was missing something. I read lots of business and strategy books, watched videos / webinars / podcasts. I took a great deal of advice, developed lots of intellectual property related to the business and did all of the reverse engineering – all amazing tools. After all of this and despite doing okay I still felt the struggle and could not find the 'x' factor.

If I am honest, I really cannot pinpoint what led me to

define what I was missing, probably a combination of lots of different elements over a period of time so I am really excited to be able to share this with you here. It was a particular coach I worked with who made it the most 'real' for me. I felt she understood me and where I was coming from. We had many things in common and various similar experiences. I identified, liked and respected her so was very open to the mindset tools she taught me. Most of the mindset work is super simple, I would really advise you not to write it off just because of the simple nature of the recommended exercises. Honestly, if you really throw yourself into this work you will see dramatic positive improvements in all areas of your life. I would absolutely love to hear how you are getting on with this work and provide additional information and support for you. Pop onto the 'Their Face, Your Business' Facebook page and let me know how things work out for you.

13 DAILY ROUTINES FOR A POSITIVE MENTAL ATTITUDE

Developing some daily habits really create a great foundation for a positive approach, improve our ability to receive good things and provide some focus; remember the 'what you focus on, you get more of' approach.

Establishing some daily routines really help create this focus from the beginning of your day, every day. Everyone will find methods of establishing and maintaining their own daily rituals as different things work for different people. To help develop your understanding of what I really mean here, I am going to take you through my own daily routines but please adapt these to make them effective in order to work best for you. Add / develop / change the techniques until you find something which is the perfect fit for your own needs.

1   First thing when I wake up is to go through all the things I am grateful for that day, often it is just simple things but it is about finding the magic in the ordinary, being grateful for my family, for my health, for my successful business; the everyday things which are actually so important to recognise and be grateful for. Sometimes I write this down, sometimes I type it or go through it on the 'notes' app on my phone, sometimes it is just a thinking exercise. The important thing is the attention you give to this; this deserves some emotional effort and will set the tone for your day. Again, if considering a whole raft of things is too much, then just focus on one, but feel into it, make it a meaningful, emotional and positive experience.

2   Review your goals. So, I have goals for the year (or at least slightly long-term), and for each week. Sometimes also I have daily goals. Each day I review these to remind myself where I am against my goal setting, tick off what I have achieved (so satisfying!) and focus on what is next on the list. Again, you create what you focus on, so this exercise is super helpful in

keeping your priorities in mind and pushing
forward to achieve them.

3   Ask yourself questions; again, this is about
    creating a positive focus. Each day I ask myself
    to remember why I love what I do, I think about
    what inspires me, who is a part of that and what
    makes us trust each other? What are my values
    and guiding principles? What is the reason I do
    what I do? I consider how I want others to
    perceive me and what I can do to be that
    person. I ask myself how I want to feel each
    day? How do I want those around me to feel
    and how can I make that happen? By all means
    choose your own key questions but making
    yourself stop and think these things through
    each day is a powerful and effective way of
    analysing our own behaviours and focusing on
    the person we want to be.

4   Affirmations; this is all about how you speak to
    yourself and creating positive powerful
    assertions which can anchor your thinking.
    These can be as simple as 'today is going to be
    fabulous,' 'it is safe for me to do well' etc. Small
    phrases which are meaningful to you can be
    really effective here. You can also use this tool
    to remind yourself and work on your weak
    points; for example, one of my daily
    affirmations is 'it is safe for me to have
    boundaries'. I know this is an area I struggle

with. By reminding myself daily that it is okay for me to have boundaries, it embeds the message in my brain day after day. This is not an overnight 'fix' but over time this message filters in, becomes embedded in our belief systems and allows us to effect change in areas of our lives where we may find it more difficult to be assertive or set boundaries for example.

5   Have a list somewhere (your phone is always a good place) of things which make you smile, the things which light you up in life. For me, my children and family are top of the list, but there are lots of other things in there too. This is something to reflect on when you are having a rough day, literally just to take a few seconds to remind yourself of the important things in your life which make you feel amazing is fabulous for stress relief. The simple act of smiling (which you will do when you read your 'smile list') is great for instantly helping you to relax. Your 'smile list' helps present some perspective around the things which are really the most important to you and helps to rationalise the things which are troubling you at the same time.

6   At the end of the day take 5 minutes to reflect. I like to ask myself 3 quick questions at the end of the day, it can be a lovely thing to do with family or friends too if you feel you can.

My 3 questions are:

i. What am I grateful for from today?
ii. Did I love as much as I could today?
iii. What do I need to clear and forgive now?

This simple exercise can be super powerful in grounding your thoughts, settling worries and for moving onto the next day in a positive and productive way.

7 Another powerful exercise is to list the top 3 people you love and really think what it is about them that you love so much. This is a brilliant exercise in appreciation. The other brilliant thing about this exercise is that those we love the most are often the ones who also drive us a little crazy! By focusing on what we love about them we learn to appreciate their fabulous qualities rather than zeroing in on the issues which irritate us the most; it gives balance and perspective. Also, as part of this exercise I often ask myself what it is I love about me. Now this I find really hard to do! Appreciating myself is often not something which feels natural for me to do and I really struggled with this at first. I do not do this every day, but when I am feeling

brave enough to really look at myself, I do and I am getting to like myself better because of it.

8   Get outside! Connecting with nature, be it a walk around the block, a run through a forest or simply standing in the garden breathing deeply, feeling the sun / wind / rain on your face and just 'being' for a few minutes is a brilliant habit to get into. This lowers your heart rate, reduces your stress levels and allows the high stress hormones to have a breather whilst you just have a moment to 'be'. For me walking or running in the countryside is just the best way of achieving this but it is not practical every day. On the occasions when it is not practical, just a few minutes of fresh air is valuable, it is something most of us can build into our day even just for a few moments and it will have a big effect on your overall wellbeing.

The above suggestions are not exhaustive, there are so many other feel good strategies you can build into your everyday life; dance in the kitchen while you are making breakfast, sing in the car on the way to work, do whatever makes you feel good in the moment and make it part of your everyday life.

Personal Experience: You have many of the tools I personally use here. My advice would be to introduce these tools over time.

As has been already mentioned, this was very much a process for me and I have built on the tools I use over quite an extended period. I suggest that employing the whole shebang all in one go might be both overwhelming and ineffective. Pick one or two tools or exercises which appeal to you. Employ those, see if they work for you (not everything will, some people swear by meditation and I am absolutely sure it can be really effective, it just does not work for me – I do not do sitting still very well)!

Keep what works for you, if it does not, move on and try another. Build up and work out your own magic formula. Then make it a habit. Set reminders to yourself to make sure you take the time every day to employ the techniques you have chosen and as ever, really feel into all of these activities. Going through the motions without the emotion just will not make the magic happen.

If you are going to do this, do it wholeheartedly; make it mean something, celebrate each experience you have along the way and enjoy the process.

14 INSPIRED ACTION

Taking action is essential, we all know this, inspired action however, is something a bit next level. Inspired action is the kind that stretches you, that scares you just a little bit, puts you out of your comfort zone and helps you feel the growing pains.

Inspired action is so much more than going through the motions of what is required on a day to day basis. It comes from your gut and your heart; it is dictated by the direction you know you want to travel but have always lacked confidence or drive to do so. Inspired action does not always need to be anything huge, it is personal, so it is the kind of achievement which may be a big deal to you whether or not it seems like a big deal to others. For some people it may be having the guts to put a picture of yourself on your website or social media page. For years, I hid behind my business logo with the tiniest picture of myself on my webpage. It took a very long time for me to have the confidence to put a proper picture of myself out there and guess what happened when I did … nothing much! By that, I mean the world did not fall apart, no-one said terrible things about me (or if they did, I did not hear them!) it was all okay. However, on that day, at that time, putting a picture of myself out there for all to see was my big, bold, scary, inspired action and I was terrified!

From there I learned to grow, not overnight, but over a period of years, I have put more and more of 'me' into my business (it is that 'like, know and trust' issue again). I have learnt, grown and most importantly developed my sense of self and my resilience, which makes taking inspired action far more exciting than it is scary these days. Now I am the face of my business, I do regular livestream videos on a variety of forums, I have been featured in the local media, done radio interviews and speak at a variety of local and national events. Each step along the way has been taken with inspired action. When I feel scared (and I do) I recognise the fear as growing pains and that in turn makes me feel excited with anticipation because feeling the growing pains mean I am getting bigger, getting better and becoming the next, new and improved, version of myself.

Personal Experience: Inspired action may sound very exciting and in many ways it is. It is also hellishly scary and can feel like you are taking an enormous risk. Often you are, but really, what is the worst that can happen?

I have had a number of experiences when I have 'put myself out there' in one form or another and been knocked back. A few years ago, this may have felt like utter rejection and sent me into the depths of despair. These days I am much more philosophical. My ideas, offers or contributions just might not fit with someone else's plans or business model and that is absolutely fine. Do not be discouraged if this happens to you. You may get an idea rejected by someone, but that someone may know someone else who a few weeks, months or even years later might remember your offer and come back to you in a way you never really expected.

My 'inspired action' has not always been big, dramatic or very public. Sometimes the inspiration comes from somewhere quieter, calmer and more in-tune with my own equilibrium. At times I have been in danger of forgetting to celebrate the small stuff, of thinking my contribution does not really matter and regressing into my 'invisible' state of hiding. I have come to realise that every little thing does matter. It is the little things which accumulate to make the big things happen and what may be a little thing to one person can be huge to someone else.

My big take home learnings have been to give myself the credit when things go right, to take the lesson when things go wrong and be very grateful for the journey whatever it looks like.

15 FEAR AND OVERWHELM

Fear is probably the single most limiting factor in stopping you from pushing forwards with your plans and progressing as you would like to.

It is insidious, working its way into every little nook and cranny, it can find to eat away at your confidence and prevent you from taking action. Bizarrely enough fear is often not recognised for what it is. We can often be too tired, too busy etc to take the action we want to take but more often than not, this is a symptom of procrastination, related to fear and it prevents us from getting into action.

I have experienced it right the way through my career,

particularly in the aesthetics field. I spent a long time being scared about people knowing I had a business (yup, great marketing strategy I know – duh!) Then I was scared about what people might think about me, I was scared of not being good enough and so it went on. It was actually more recently than probably I would care to admit, that I finally saw my procrastination for what it was ... fear! I tell you what though, recognising fear and naming it was utterly liberating. Once I understood and appreciated that I was just scared, I could go through my grounding exercises, undertake some of my 'feel good now' strategies and all of a sudden, I had more resilience and cared much less about what others thought of me. I could name the fear, recognise the growing pains, get excited about taking the next big, scary step and move forwards.

Overwhelm often comes after the fear (but is probably fear's close cousin anyway). Overwhelm often hits just before a period of rapid growth. You have done your feel-good work, you are grounded, you are out in nature, and you are taking your inspired action and 'bam' it hits you, there is just too much to do, so little time, you do not know what to prioritise. You hit overwhelm and feel utterly swamped with all the demands on your time, all the things you have to think about, the deadlines you have to meet, you can lose the joy, you do not feel good and procrastination can, once again, rear its ugly head.

The important thing here is to recognise what is actually going on, to slow down and set the priorities. Find yourself some joy, give yourself a little time to settle, to think and to get a little creative. Again, time outside, exercise, singing, dancing, cuddling a baby, walking the dog whatever brings you calmness is a brilliant idea here. Create manageable timescales for the tasks you have prioritised and focus on these first. Celebrate every task achieved and try to relax into the process.

At all times, but particularly in times of overwhelment and fear (or even overwhelming fear), learn to prioritise the sacred 'top three' things while you ride out the storm:

1   Exercise; we all know that a healthy body and healthy mind go hand in hand. Physical activity is a great way of burning off nervous energy and can help calm a busy mind. Twenty minutes or so of exercise three times a week is a great start, you do not have to be a committed gym goer, any activity is good.

2   Nutrition; at times of high emotion is so very easy to comfort eat. To help manage physical stress good nutrition is key; feed your body, not your emotions and you will not go far wrong.

3   Sleep; worry, stress, fear, the whole range of negative emotions can play havoc with our sleep. Making sleep a priority at these times is so important. There are many studies which highlight the importance of good quality sleep of a good duration eg 7-8 hours to manage stress and improve our productivity. Try to safeguard your sleep routine, keep away from screens for one hour before bed, keep away from caffeine, make sure your room is calm and dark. Do all the things necessary for your body and your mind to recognise that now is the time for sleep. Go to bed and stay there even if sleep eludes you. Training your body to rest can be a challenge for those of us who struggle to relax. Creating the right environment and accepting that, awake or asleep, you are staying there until morning helps establish a good sleep routine. Commit to it and things will improve over time.

Get the above three things in order and the feelings of overwhelm and fear become much easier to recognise and manage.

Another strategy for managing negative emotions, particularly fear, is to reframe the feeling in a different way. There are many circumstances when fear can be the default feeling; when trying to meet a deadline, before an exam, in all sorts of high stress environments. In these cases, I find it really useful to reframe my fear as excitement. This is not 'playing pretend' it is seeing beyond the fear. For example, I may be scared because of an upcoming exam or excited because this exam is a step forward into the next big challenge. I remember being terrified before I did my first livestream video but by changing my view from fear to anticipation and excitement I could come across as positive rather than fearful, thereby creating a positive experience for anyone watching and a much better experience for myself.

Seeing fear and overwhelment as symptoms of growth and development is a really constructive way forward. I have talked about feeling the 'growing pains' (which is what these feelings are) earlier in this book. Recognising the growing pains and being grateful for them is another helpful exercise. Being grateful that you are achieving your goals, moving forward and developing is a powerful way of managing fear and overwhelm. It is a way of seeing past the difficult emotions, by being thankful for the growing pains and being excited for what is to come. This beats back the fear and opens you up to hopefulness, excitement and personal growth.

Personal Experience: Quiet honestly, if there was a specialist subject around fear and overwhelm, I would win 'Mastermind' with it. Fear and overwhelm are great friends of mine and it is only in the last few years that I have made up my mind that we absolutely have to break up! Even then, this debilitating duo still keep showing up from time to time and I can struggle to show them the door. They can draw me in and I can get totally caught up in the emotional panic they create. It is not a healthy relationship but when they show up at times and I am feeling vulnerable, I can be terribly guilty of swinging the door wide and welcoming them in. It is not good; it has to stop and I am winning this break-up battle, slowly, deliberately and one feel good technique at a time!

I have mentioned that exercise is a great stress relief technique for me and running is my weapon of choice. I have actually done some of my longest runs and best times, at the worst times in my life. I went through an extended period of stress in the years before I ventured into Aesthetics, due to a toxic work environment. I genuinely have that to thank for some of the best runs I have ever done! That awful experience also taught me how to manage my stress levels, set my boundaries and find things to be grateful for which take the focus away from the circumstances which were destroying my sense of self, my already limited self-confidence and my overall effectiveness.

I am hoping anyone reading this book is not in a place quite so destructive to their sense of self, but it happens all the time and this is the stuff that fear and overwhelm feed, grow and flourish on. It is hard to be grateful for an experience if it pulls you in on a downward spiral. That is why it is so important to have your feel-good strategies at your fingertips, to build your resilience with these tools, to do some boundary setting (next chapter) and to have goals and a sense of direction. Alongside this, set your milestones and celebrate the wins, big or small at every opportunity.

16 SETTING BOUNDRIES

A really excellent way of mitigating for overwhelm (and a whole host of other draining situations) is all around establishing boundaries. So often you can become swamped, distracted, stressed and overburdened because you do not have firm, established boundaries. Taking too much on, or prioritising everything, is a recipe for disaster and the chances are your productivity will suffer. Scheduling your priorities helps to create structure and reinforces your limits.

Another way in which boundaries may need to be established is related to the behaviour you will accept from others. This is an area which I have particularly struggled with. I am sure I am not alone in this as there are so many people, I have spoken with over the years, whose biggest challenge is setting and maintaining boundaries and related standards around their own and others expectations. When others have expectations of you (be it what you do, or in the way they feel they are allowed to treat you) which is beyond what you can manage, you are going to run into trouble. Ultimately, you lose your feel-good vibe which then negatively impacts in all areas of your business, social and home life.

With this in mind, here are my top tips for establishing and maintaining firm boundaries:

- Figure out what you are happy to do, the limits of your responsibilities, your core values and write them down. This process allows you to really think about what has been bothering you from a positive 'what I can do' perspective. It takes the focus off the negative whilst still creating boundaries.

- Do the same with how you expect people to treat you. If you are experiencing unacceptable behaviour, be clear with yourself regarding what your expectations and limits are, what you value most and how you treat other people in relation to how you expect them to treat you in return. Again, try to frame this in a positive 'what I expect' manner rather than a 'what I won't accept' exercise.

- Write yourself some affirmations eg 'I deserve to be treated with kindness and respect' or 'I prioritise my family time'. Go over these every day, spend time feeling into it, what will that family time look like? What emotions come up just thinking about that? Feel the positives as if it were real right now. This is a brilliant technique to use before kindly, but firmly saying something like 'I am afraid I have other pressing priorities right now, I cannot commit to 'x''. It helps build confidence in your decision making and makes the kind but firm boundary setting much easier to achieve.

- A handy little trick I learned from a lovely friend is great for managing people who 'overstep the mark' in terms of how they treat you. The trick is simply to listen to what is being said and then ask 'I didn't quite catch that; can you repeat it please?' This is like holding a mirror up to the other person. If you are asked to repeat something, you have to think about what you are saying. Very often this simple technique alone, will make people really stop and think about what they are saying and realise they may have crossed a line. It also provides you with a few moments to gather your thoughts and emotions to give a calm and kind but firm response, rather than giving a knee-jerk reaction which you may regret later.

- Be consistent. Once you have some clarity on what you expect of yourself and from other people, practice kindly, but firmly, enforcing your boundaries consistently. This is so important. If people feel you have flexibility with your boundaries, they will constantly push, and you will constantly be stressed and overwhelmed and the whole exercise will be a waste. One of my clinical boundaries is that I will only use the high-end products. Unless my products have FDA approval, clinical trials and masses of research-based evidence, it is not the product for me. My patients know this and respect me for it (the boundary actually attracts my ideal patient and puts off those looking for a cheap deal). Now imagine if I was completely inconsistent with this approach. My patient's may not be sure of the quality or providence of the product they are receiving, I wouldn't be attracting my 'ideal patient' so probably would not have the wonderful relationships I have with my ladies and gents, my business model would be vague and my appeal would be diluted. My business would suffer and so would I. This is only one example, but you can see how once you have set your boundaries, committing to them and being consistent is so important. It can be tough at first, people will 'rattle the cage to see if the bars have moved' but please do not let them; toughing it out in the short term will pay dividends in the long run.

- Employ all your feel-good strategies to get you through this transitional phase. Keep focused on the outcomes you imagined in step 1, be kind, be consistent and balance will emerge.

Of course, this advice is only helpful when you are dealing with normal, reasonable situations and reasonably healthy relationships. For anyone in an abusive situation the advice would be very different and in these cases I absolutely recommend seeking professional advice, help and support.

Personal Experience: I have always been the kind of person who operates with a high degree of tolerance. I put up with a lot until someone reaches 'the line' with me, at which point, I am done. There is nothing really wrong with this approach but over the last few years I have re-evaluated and tried to be clear about my boundaries and enforcing them sooner. The problem with the 'high tolerance' model is that it does not really give a clear message. The reason people pushed and pushed with me, is because I let them. Then when I had had enough, I really had nothing left to give. Depending on the circumstances I have been physically and emotionally wrung out by this approach and the other party has not really understood what the problem is. Their behaviour towards me, may have been unacceptable, but because I allowed it to continue, they did not know my feelings on the subject.

As someone who also shies away from confrontation, this can be a very difficult nut to crack. Boundaries, however, are the answer. Be clear from the very beginning of any relationship be it with a patient, a family member or partner, what your expectations are and what they can expect from you. If it helps, write this down. From a clinical perspective many of your boundaries will be in your consent form which the patient signs and is legally bound to; make sure they are. It can be simple issues about your follow-up care or 'adjustment' dose appointments; do you offer these, at what timescales from the original treatment would you undertake this procedure, how many follow-up appointments do you offer?

I am happy to report, that these days, I am much better at my boundary setting. I have limits on the ages of patients I will treat for example (this has always been non-negotiable, from the very beginning of my aesthetics life) usually my patients are over the age of 25 and I never, ever treat anyone younger than 18. If I feel patients have unrealistic expectations, despite my best efforts to educate and inform, I will choose not to treat them. If I feel that a patient is asking for a 'look' I am not comfortable to create I will not treat them. In fact, at my initial patient meeting, I introduce myself and am very clear about my ethics, my approach and what I will and will not do in terms of treatments and looks. It is an approach I find really effective and patients respect my honesty and my boundaries. It is a skill though and has taken some time to learn, develop and hone into a fine art. In the early days I was less confident, shied away from these honest conversations and ended up doing many free treatments because I had not met the patient's expectations; it is not good for business, self-confidence or your patients to take this approach. If you are just starting out now, please learn from my mistakes and avoid the heartache of finding this out the hard way!

17 REFRESH, REFLECT AND RENEW

Periods of significant growth are cyclical. They take, effort, emotion, hard work and masses of energy. This growth phase is not sustainable long term, we would all burn out eventually!

After periods of high activity and development, it is really important to take some time, to settle, to reflect, relax and rest in preparation for the next cycle. Individuals vary in their needs regarding the length of the ideal cycle and the related rest periods individuals require afterwards vary considerably. I know my personal threshold falls in approximately 3-month cycles and I need about 3 weeks of downtime between each. For me growth and development (be it personal or business) requires time, effort, commitment and lots of high activity. It is exciting, rewarding, fulfilling and brings me joy ... it also makes me very tired towards the end of a high activity cycle, so rest is a must. Again, for me, it takes about a week or so to settle and relax after a period of intense productivity and I need a further 2 weeks to re-energise and to get the creative juices flowing again. Notably, it is during my downtime that a lot of my inspiration comes to me regarding the next steps and new developments. It is an absolute essential part of my personal development journey. By the end of my 3 weeks, I am chomping at the bit, ready to get started again!

The process is different for everyone so it is really important to become familiar with what works for you, to recognise your own needs and respect them too. Schedule some fun time into your periods of high activity so you keep uplifted and manage your energies well, but equally plan in your down time and allow yourself to relax, reward yourself for the growth you have experienced and for what is coming next, you are on your way!

Personal Experience: It took me a while to learn this lesson too! One of my strengths is that I can be very focused and have good self-discipline. It is a great strength to have and harness … in the right context. However, taken to the extreme in conjunction with goal setting, moving forwards and business development it can also drive me into the ground! Years ago, I moved into a rented property which was in a state of cosmetic dis-repair. The landlord cut me a deal that, if I decorated the whole place (a 3-bedroom semi-detached house) I could have the first month rent free.

Partly I was daft enough to be pressured into renting a property which was far too big for one person (yup, that boundary thing again) and partly I was so driven to get the place looking nice that I set myself a grueling decorating timetable, running alongside my demanding full-time job. I worked all hours of the day and night to achieve my schedule. I did have some help (bless my Mum and Dad) but I did not want to burden them too much with a commitment I had made, so, the bulk of the work I did myself. I totally denied myself any down-time until the task was complete (and honestly, the place was a pit, it was a big task). I literally made myself ill in the process.

The downtime eventually arrived when I had successfully made myself so ill, I earned myself a hospital bed for the week. Not my brightest moment but a big lesson in time management, goal setting, scheduling and allowing myself some time to rest.

Relaxing, in the sense of not doing much, is still something I struggle to do. I have never really got into the 'Spa Day' thing which is so popular and I am honestly quite jealous of those who can truly relax and embrace the concept of doing nothing; it just is not me.

These days however, I have learned to recognise the signs that I need to slow down (they usually show up as anxiety and overwhelm usually when I am on a mission to achieve a specific target and have not allowed myself the time I need to mitigate for managing my energies). Whilst I still have a way to go, in terms of planning in the time I require to avoid tripping over the overwhelment and anxiety issues, once they do show up, I am getting better at recognising them and managing myself to loosen their influence and grip on my reality. As ever, for me, exercise is always my first starting point to get rid of the nervous energy. Quality family time really helps me too; there is nothing better than spending time making memories with the people you love the most. Finally, time alone is essential for me. At heart I am an absolute introvert. I love spending time with people and have worked hard to 'put myself out there' to support and grow my business. I have succeeded so well on that score now that I truly enjoy speaking at events, meeting new people, being challenged and challenging others, supporting, guiding, training, mentoring, coaching – the whole bit, I love it all! However, at the end of the day I need the time alone to reflect, to settle, to refresh my energies and renew myself for the next big challenge.

If this resonates with you, I suggest you try to do something similar. By allowing yourself this prescribed downtime in your schedule, you are bringing your best version of yourself to every part of your life. Your business will thank you and so will your family. After all, our family are often who we are doing this all for. There are no shortcuts, it is hard work, but with the right combination of focus, goals, drive, mindset tools, permitted reflection and downtime there is an easier way to make it all work; I encourage everyone to find their own magic formula!

18 KEEP IN TOUCH

Thank you so much for taking the time to read this book, it would be lovely to hear from you if you would like to ask questions, give feedback or comments or have any other contributions. Email; tracey@eastridingma.uk or find me on Facebook; Tracey Dennison; Aesthetics Nurse, Trainer, Mentor and Mindset Coach

If you are a medical professional within the Aesthetics Industry or involved in the business side of the industry, feel free to join our Facebook community which offers regular content around growth and development within the Aesthetics Industry. We have a variety of online tools as well as occasional free workshops and masterminds. The link is; https://www.facebook.com/groups/655407244944345/about/

We have an online teaching module available for those

developing in the Aesthetics world. This can be found at: https://www.udemy.com/course/starting-your-business-in-medical-aesthetics/learn/lecture/17253360#overview

Keep an eye on Udemy for further coaching modules coming soon.

19 ADDITIONAL RECOMMENDED READING/LISTENING

I am delighted to have been able to introduce you to some of the elements and key concepts required for developing in Medical Aesthetics. Listed below is some further reading or listening (got to love an audiobook!) which has helped and inspired me in my business and personal development if you would also like to take a look!

Girl on Fire - Cara Alwill Leyba

The Universe Has Your Back – Gabrielle Bernstein

High Performance Habits – Brendan Burchard

The Art of Being Brilliant – Andy Cope and Andy Whittaker

Changing Faces – Richard Crawford-Small

The Secret – Rhonda Byrne

The Magic – Rhonda Byrne

Get Rich Lucky Bitch – Denise Duffield-Thomas

The Big Leap – Gay Hendricks

Good Vibes, Good Life – Vex King

The One Thing – Gary Keller, Jay Papasan

The Chimp Paradox – Steve Peters

Oversubscribed – Daniel Priestley

Entrepreneur Revolution – Daniel Priestley

24 Assets – Daniel Priestley

Awaken the Giant Within – Tony Robins

Start with Why – Simon Sinek

You are a Badass – Jen Sincero

You are a Badass at Making Money – Jen Sincero

A Mindfulness Guide for the Frazzled – Ruby Wax

ABOUT THE AUTHOR

Tracey Dennison: Advanced Aesthetics Nurse Director, Trainer, Mentor and Coach.

Tracey has been in Nursing for 27 years and has been in Aesthetics since 2014. She has striven to continually develop her knowledge, skills and expertise and has undertaken extensive amounts of training to facilitate this.

Tracey is the Nurse Director of East Riding Aesthetics which offers a full range of Aesthetic injectable treatments, she is also an Aesthetics Trainer, Mentor and Coach attracting students from all over England to her training and internationally for her online coaching work.

What inspired Tracey to enter the world of coaching was the realisation that mindset work and personal development is critical to business success. Having been on this journey of self-development herself and experienced first-hand the huge impact this approach can have both personally and in business, Tracey feels it is important to share the secrets of an abundant business mindset to help, support and inspire others to achieve and build on their own business models. Tracey is always happy to hear from those wanting to grow and develop in their own business and can be contacted on: tracey@eastridingma.uk